A GIFT FOR:

_____

FROM:

_____

*If I can find in myself a desire*

*which no experience in the world can satisfy,*

*the most probable explanation is*

*that I was made for another world.*

—C. S. LEWIS

*You never lose someone*
*when you know where to find them*

# Heaven

## BILL & GLORIA
## GAITHER
### & Friends

J. COUNTRYMAN®
NASHVILLE, TENNESSEE
www.jcountryman.com

Project Editor: Kathy Baker

Design: Kirk DouPonce, UDG | DesignWorks, Sisters, Oregon

ISBN 0–8499–9592–2

Printed and bound in Belgium

www.thomasnelson.com
www.jcountryman.com

And this is the promise

that He has promised us—

—I JOHN 2:25

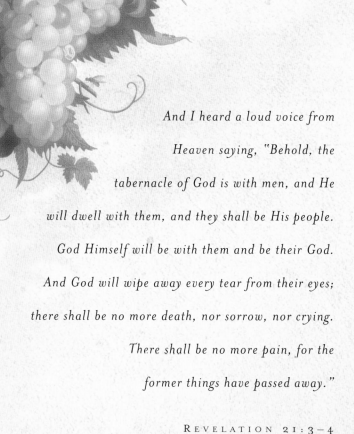

And I heard a loud voice from
Heaven saying, "Behold, the
tabernacle of God is with men, and He
will dwell with them, and they shall be His people.
God Himself will be with them and be their God.
And God will wipe away every tear from their eyes;
there shall be no more death, nor sorrow, nor crying.
There shall be no more pain, for the
former things have passed away."

REVELATION 21:3–4

HEAVEN—*God's Precious Promise*

HEAVEN—*Home of Our Hopes*

HEAVEN—*Here & Now*

HEAVEN—*The Glory of God!*

# *God's Precious Promise*

eaven. Home. That destination beyond what our eyes can see. It's been on the minds of poets, philosophers, and preachers for millenia.

In his play *Our Town*, Thornton Wilder approaches the subject this way: "We all know that something is eternal. And it ain't houses and it ain't names, and it ain't earth, and it ain't even the stars . . . everybody knows in their bones that something is eternal."

No matter how tragic or triumphant your life may be, you somehow can hear the inner whisper that tells you there must be something more, something better than anything you've ever known. It's a longing for Heaven, a quiet ache that feels a little like being homesick, like being caught between the now and the not—yet.

In 2002, many of our Homecoming Friends gathered to consider what "going home" means, to share the writings of our most cherished thinkers, and to sing songs that invite glimpses of Heaven. This book is an outpouring of that intense, worshipful experience.

Heaven is the ultimate reality we all must face. This world is not our home. We are just passing through. So come with us as we explore Heaven. It's where we belong. Forever!

*This world is not conclusion,*

*A sequel stands beyond,*

*Invisible as music, But positive as sound.*

—EMILY DICKINSON

Dear God,

May Your love and understanding fill the hearts of

everyone who reads this book. May each page

guide them deeper into Your hope.

May the grieving or fearful receive Your comfort,

may the seekers find Your answer,

and may the confident celebrate anew the joy of

Your promised Heaven. In Jesus' Name,

Home of our
Hopes

*In talking about Heaven,*

*Peter Marshall said,*

*"Those we love are*

*with the Lord, and the Lord*

*has promised to be with us.*

*If they are with Him,*

*and He is with us,*

*they can't be far away."*

# What We Anticipate

*H*ave you ever sipped fresh, cool lemonade underneath a tree on a sweltering afternoon? Or savored the first unhindered stretch when you got your cast off? Those are tastes of Heaven.

Have you ever embraced your best friend after a long time apart? Do you remember swinging in your daddy's arms or reading books on the floor with Mom? You've experienced bits of Heaven's joy.

What about those rare, perfect days when you had so much fun, when you felt great and full of energy, and when everything went just exactly right? Every day in Heaven will be far better.

Heaven is the home of our hopes, and on the following pages are some of what we're looking forward to the most.

# HOPE

GLORIA GAITHER, 2002

*The hope that is within us,*
*Erupting from the sand,*
*Is clear and pure refreshment*
*In dry and barren land;*
*No scorching circumstances*
*Can stop the eager flow*
*Of Hope that springs eternal—*
*This Joy that floods my soul.*

*You cannot make it happen—*
*Like faith, it is a gift—*
*The currents of depression*
*The power of Hope will lift.*
*Just when you least expect it*
*A rescue raft comes by*
*And ties your weary spirit*
*To wings so you can fly!*

*Hope that sometimes whispers—*
*A Hope that sometimes shouts—*
*Sometimes Hope's mighty gale*
*Will part the sea of doubts.*
*Hope calms the raging fevers,*
*Commands the storms of pain;*
*Hope turns life's threatening tempest*
*To gentle, soothing rain.*

*Oh Jesus, blessed Jesus,*
*My wellspring in the sand—*
*Oh Jesus, blessed Jesus,*
*My strong and saving hand—*
*Oh Jesus, blessed Jesus,*
*My anchored tether—rope—*
*The voice that stills all rages,*
*My shouting, whispering Hope!*

# Reunion & Rejoicing

## When All of God's Singers Get Home

GLORIA GAITHER

I like to think that before time began, before the world was created or galaxies flung into space, there was God—and He was singing a song. The music was so beautiful that it had to be heard. So God created . . . and down through the ages He's always had His singers who picked up the fragments of the melody, hummed bits of harmony, wrote phrases of poetry, or danced short movements. No one has ever heard the whole song since that day God sang it alone. But one of these days He will gather all His children home, and one by one the singers of all the ages will lift their voices and fill in the parts life taught to them. At last we'll hear love's sweetest song as it was first conceived in the heart of the great song writer Himself. It will be perfect. What music there will be when the song of the ages is sung around the Father's throne when all of God's singers get home!

# WHEN WE
# ALL GET TO HEAVEN

ELIZA E. HEWITT, 1898

*Sing the wondrous love of Jesus,*
*Sing His mercy and His grace.*
*In the mansions bright and blessèd*
*He'll prepare for us a place.*

*When we all get to heaven,*
*What a day of rejoicing that will be!*
*When we all see Jesus,*
*We'll sing and shout the victory!*

Having grown up in church and in a gospel music family, I have heard and sung songs about Heaven all my life. Recently they started having a little more impact as we buried my dad. Just to have his heritage and his legacy has been wonderful, but to know where he is today because the Bible says, "though I am absent from you in body I am present with you in spirit" (Colossians 2:5). That gives me great comfort to know that even though I miss him here, I will spend eternity with him. The separation would be unbearable if I didn't know I would see him again, but I know I will some day.

— BILLY BLACKWOOD

*You are no longer strangers and foreigners, but fellow citizens with the saints and members of the household of God.*

— EPHESIANS 2:19

When you start making deposits into Heaven, it starts to become more real.

— BABBIE MASON

*He shall call to the heavens from above,*
*And to the earth, that He may judge His people:*
*"Gather My saints together to Me,*
*Those who have made a covenant with Me by sacrifice."*
*Let the heavens declare His righteousness,*
*For God Himself is Judge. Selah.*

— PSALM 50:4—6

There are a lot of people who say to me, "Joni, being in that wheelchair, I bet you just can't wait for Heaven." Don't assume that all I ever do is dream of springing up out of this wheelchair. No, I am looking forward to Heaven because of a new heart, a heart free of sin, and sorrow, and selfishness. Even though I would enjoy jumping up, kicking, dancing, and doing aerobics, having a new heart beats having a new body any day.

—JONI EARECKSON TADA

When I was younger, Heaven seemed like a fairy–tale kingdom, an imaginary place where everything was great and wonderful—no pain, no sorrow, no sickness. And it still is all those things, but for me now it is a totally different thing. I lost my mom very unexpectedly, and I have a sister and other family members in Heaven. Now Heaven is my connection to them. It is the thread of hope that I hang on to knowing that our relationship is not over.

—LADYE LOVE SMITH

The only comfort there is when you lose a loved one is in turning to the Lord. The harder we try to work to figure it out for ourselves, the worse off we get. You have just got to trust in God and know that everything is going to be all right someday.

—JAKE HESS

People we love don't always leave this earth with every dispute settled, every important message delivered, every pardon asked for and received. My husband, Russ, lost his father a few years ago, and in the words of song we later wrote, "They loved each other so very much, but not so very well." They didn't have the chance for a final conversation, so Russ was left with the full weight of his grief and also of their unfinished business. In the years since then, I've watched Russ slowly begin to let go of the pain of that loss, but it never really goes away. I'm sure our Heavenly Father understands that yearning, that need for reconciliation, His own Son died for it. But what do you do if it's too late? I believe in a Heaven where our human frailties and mistakes and all the pain we cause each other because of them will not only be forgiven, but healed and forgotten, tossed into the sea of forgetfulness once and for all. I believe in a Heaven that has a quiet corner somewhere waiting for Russ and his dad so they can sit down face to face and finally have that talk. I believe in a Heaven so infused with the loving presence of God that even the sadness of a broken relationship will grow strangely dim in the light of His glory and grace.

— TORI TAFF

*I will praise You forever,*
*Because You have done it;*
*And in the presence of Your saints*
*I will wait on Your name, for it is good*

— PSALM 52:9

# SHOULD YOU GO FIRST
## AND I REMAIN

BY ALBERT ROWSWELL

*Should you go first and I remain to walk the road alone,*
*I'll live in memory's garden, dear, with happy days we've known.*
*In spring I'll watch for roses red when fades the lilac blue,*
*And in early fall when brown leaves call, I'll catch a glimpse of you.*

*Should you go first and I remain for battles to be fought,*
*Each thing you've touched along the way will be a hallowed spot.*
*I'll hear your voice, I'll see your smile and though blindly I may grope,*
*The memory of your helping hand will bore me on with hope.*

*Should you go first and I remain, one thing I'd have you do:*
*Walk slowly down that long, long path for soon I'll follow you.*
*And I'll want to know each step you take that I may walk the same,*
*For someday down that lonely road you'll hear me call your name.*

# BEYOND THE SUNSET

VIRGIL P. BROCK, BLANCHE KERR BROCK, 1936

*Beyond the sunset, O blissful morning,*
*When with our Savior Heaven is begun;*
*Earth's toiling ended, O glorious dawning,*
*Beyond the sunset, when day is done.*

*Beyond the sunset no clouds will gather,*
*No storms will threaten, no fears annoy;*
*O day of gladness, O day unending,*
*Beyond the sunset, eternal joy!*

*Beyond the sunset, O glad reunion,*
*With our dear loved ones who've gone before;*
*In that fair homeland we'll know no parting,*
*Beyond the sunset forevermore!*

Two of my favorite Bible passages are Psalm 139:16, which clearly says that my death date is determined long before my birth date, and the other is Isaiah 57:1–2, which explains that the godly die young because God sees the trouble that lies ahead of them. When our oldest daughter at age forty–six went home to be with the Lord, I found extraordinary comfort in those two assurances. We had done everything we could humanly speaking to prolong her life. We gave her the best medical care, the most love, and the most affirmation that you could imagine, and yet God had her death date measured. Knowing that her life now is total and complete, absolutely perfect because it's with the Lord, and knowing that we will see her again, oh what a comfort that is. We do worship a great God.

—ZIG ZIGLAR

My good friend Bob Benson used to imagine all earthly goodbyes ending with the simple phrase, "See you at the House." I can still hear him say that.

—BILL GAITHER

As glorious as is our hope of seeing Christ face to face, Heaven is more. Heaven will be to join with the redeemed of all ages in singing Handel's Hallelujah Chorus.

—WILLIAM GREATHOUSE

# LOOK FOR ME
### RUSTY GOODMAN, 1982

*When you finally make your entrance to that city*
*Of jasper walls and bright golden avenues*
*As you behold all its beauty and its splendor*
*Remember there is just one request I make of you.*

*Look for me, for I will be there, too*
*I realize when you arrive there'll be so much to do*
*After you've been there ten thousand years, a million, maybe two*
*Look for me, for I will be there, too.*

# KNOWING YOU'LL BE THERE

SUZANNE JENNINGS, MICHAEL SYKES, 2002

*The other day*
*I passed the place you always liked to go*
*And I picked up the phone because*
*I thought you'd want to know*
*But I forgot you weren't there*
*I miss you on those days*
*That I'm reminded of your smile*
*And the funny things you'd say*

*Knowing we can spend a lifetime*
*Reminiscing on the past*
*Knowing I will see your face again*
*Where tender moments last*
*It makes me want to go there*
*Knowing I won't be alone*
*Knowing you'll be there*
*Makes it easy to go home*

# Understanding, Healing & Belonging

Heaven will be a place of total love, total acceptance, and total honesty. Those are the things that hold us back the most here, because we don't feel accepted and are inadequate at accepting others. Even in our relationships, we often think the worst; the less we understand the more we can hate. Heaven will be total understanding and total love.

—GLORIA GAITHER

Being born with cerebral palsy like I am, one thing I tell my four children is that when we get to Heaven, Daddy is going to have a brand new body. I am not going to walk with a limp anymore. I am not going to talk like I do anymore. We are all going to walk and talk like He does.

—DAVID RING

As an African–American living in America, I will finally have a home where I really belong. I've gone to Africa and I know that is the origin of my people, but it is really not my home. I know that my people were brought to America under the circumstances of slavery and so really this is not my home. But when I get to Heaven, I will be in a place where I really belong. And it will be good to be home.

—BABBIE MASON

*Then He who sat on the throne said, "Behold, I make all things new."*
*. . . And He said to me, "It is done! I am the Alpha and the Omega,*
*the Beginning and the End. I will give of the fountain of the water of*
*life freely to him who thirsts."*

—REVELATION 21:5–6

Heaven is the place where we become complete. We all have this feeling of inadequacy or self–conscious or longing to be more than we are. This life is just preparation for that place of completeness and fullness. That is why we get little glimpses of it every once in awhile too, when we actually are around some place or event or people where the Kingdom breaks in and we see reconciliation, or we see somebody actually repent, or forgiveness take place. That process is remarkable and so against our human nature—it is the type of stuff that beckons us home.

— BUDDY GREENE

# I Don't Belong
## (Sojourner's Song)
### Gloria Gaither, Buddy Greene, 1990

*It's not home where men sell their souls*
*And the taste of power is sweet*
*Where wrong is right and neighbors fight*
*While the hungry are dying in the street*
*Where kids are abused and women are used*
*And the weak are crushed by the strong*
*Nations gone mad, Jesus is sad.*
*And I don't belong*

*I don't belong and I'm going someday*
*Home to my own native land*
*I don't belong and it seems like I hear*
*The sound of a welcome home band*
*I don't belong, well I'm a foreigner here*
*Just singing a sojourner's song*
*I've always known this place ain't home*
*And I don't belong*

Heaven is God's home where all has been put right, where everybody belongs, where everybody is experiencing love to its fullest—the love that God has for them and the love that spills over to each other. That love will create music, dancing, and art with reckless abandon, because we will finally get over ourselves and our insecurities and all those things. Heaven will be so glorious!

—BUDDY GREENE

*He who has begun a good work in you will complete it until the day of Jesus Christ.*

—PHILIPPIANS 1:6

Russ Taff and I went to visit a prostitute from the streets of Nashville who was dying in state custody down at the hospital. The brokenness and sadness of the world had seemed to have landed on her like terrorism, and her seventy–five–pound frame was crumbling underneath it. As the weeks passed and she began to draw some of her last breaths, I had a vision of Heaven—she soon would be lying in the arms of our Lord, weeping no more. The Lord would weep instead for all the hell and brokenness and pain we cause each other here on earth.

—BECCA STEVENS

*There is a special rest still waiting for the people of God. For all who enter into God's rest will find rest from their labors, just as God rested after creating the world.*

—HEBREWS 4:9–10, NLT

There's a wonderful story told of an old American missionary named Samuel Morrison. He'd been in Africa for twenty-five years serving the Lord. Because of illness and old age they were sending him home to America. He traveled home on the same ocean liner on which President Theodore Roosevelt was coming home from a safari. As the ship pulled into New York Harbor it looked like all of America had turned out to welcome President Roosevelt home. The bands were playing, flags were waving, balloons were popping, and all the cameramen were there. When they put the gangway down to the dock, there was a thunderous ovation as everybody welcomed Mr. President home. When Samuel Morrison stepped off of the ship onto that same gangway, nobody called his name. When he walked through the crowd, there was nobody there to welcome him. He was standing on the curb looking for a cab, and in his spirit he was complaining. He said, "God, Mr. Roosevelt has been in Africa for three weeks killing animals and the whole world turns out to welcome him home. And I've been in Africa twenty–five years serving You, and there's no one here to welcome me." And he said that to his heart came that still small voice, "But My son, you're not Home yet."

—ANNE GRAHAM LOTZ

# SWEET BEULAH LAND

### SQUIRE PARSONS, 1979

*I'm kind of homesick,*
*Homesick for that country*
*To which I've never been before*
*No sad goodbyes will there be spoken*
*For time won't matter anymore*

*Beulah Land, I'm longing for you*
*And someday on thee I'll stand*
*There my heart shall be eternal*
*Beulah Land, sweet Beulah Land*

Anne Graham Lotz writes in her book *Heaven, My Father's House*:

Heaven will not only look fresh and new, it will feel fresh and new. John gives us not just a vision of Heaven's fresh beauty but a "feel" of Heaven's serenity, which permeates the atmosphere because God is there: "And I heard a loud voice from the throne saying, 'Now the dwelling of God is with men, and He will live with them, they will be His people, and God Himself will be with them and be their God. He will wipe every tear from their eyes. There will be no more death or mourning or crying or pain for the old order of things has passed away'" (Revelation 21:3–4). In what way are you suffering? Are you suffering physically, emotionally, mentally, financially, materially, relationally, socially, spiritually? One day God Himself will take your face in His hands and gently wipe away your tears as He reassures you that there will be no more suffering in My Father's House. No more pain, or hospitals, or death, or funerals, or grief, or walkers, or canes, or wheelchairs. There will be no more suicide bombers or fiery infernos, broken homes or broken hearts, broken lives or broken dreams. There will be no more mental retardation or physical handicaps, muscular dystrophy or multiple sclerosis, blindness or lameness, deafness or sickness. There will be no more Parkinson's disease or heart disease, diabetes or arthritis, cataracts or paralysis. No more cancer or strokes or AIDS. No more guns in schools, or car bombs, or terrorists, or missiles, or air strikes. No more war! You can look forward with hope, because one day there will be no more separation, no more scars, no more suffering in My Father's House. It's the home of your dreams!

# Being With Jesus

Jesus said, "Today you will be with Me in paradise" (Luke 23:43)—and the angels looked to see who would be the first one He would take to paradise.

—BILLY GRAHAM

My view of Heaven from childhood came from hearing a preacher talk about golden streets and mansions, the crystal sea, and all the things we tend to picture in our minds. As I get older when I think of Heaven, I think of the people who are there and the fact that it will be my opportunity to be with them again. I think about having a conversation with this Person to whom I have given my life, to actually encounter Him and ask Him some questions.

—JANET PASCHAL

*For at the right time Christ will be revealed from Heaven by the blessed and only almighty God, the King of kings and Lord of lords. He alone can never die, and he lives in light so brilliant that no human can approach him. No one has ever seen him, nor ever will. To him be honor and power forever. Amen.*

—1 TIMOTHY 6:15–16 NLT

I have friends in Heaven, but I think the most important thing about Heaven is seeing the Father face to face. To me, if there were no walls of jasper or pearls or anything else, just seeing God is going to be the ultimate. We will join with the angels and worship God. I can't wait until we actually get to be in that worship service.

—SARAH DELANE

*And being found in appearance as a man, He humbled Himself and became obedient to the point of death, even the death of the cross. Therefore God also has highly exalted Him and given Him the name which is above every name, that at the name of Jesus every knee should bow, of those in heaven, and of those on earth, and of those under the earth, and that every tongue should confess that Jesus Christ is Lord, to the glory of God the Father.*

—PHILIPPIANS 2:8–11

Do you ever wonder what your loved ones who have gone on to Heaven are doing? My dad often prayed, "Lord Jesus, would You pick my father out of the crowd and pull him up to Your side, and put Your arm around him, and tell him we love him." And it's so funny after the prayer because Dad always said, "Don't you know Grandpa was surprised when Jesus said, 'Come here,' put His arm around him, and told him He loves him—and that we do too."

—MARK LOWRY

There's a chorus that most everybody knows. And it brings to my mind every time, thoughts about Heaven. At some of these times, I began to think about what Heaven is like. It's common to think about being with loved ones who've gone on there ahead of you—your mother maybe, your father, or others. But for me the crowning attraction of Heaven is that it is a home that Jesus told us He is preparing for us, the place that we will share with Him. He is with us here, too, as He promised, but then we will see Him face to face.

*What a day that will be when my Savior finds me*
*I shall look upon the face of One who saved me by His grace.*
*And He'll take me by the hand and lead me to the Promised Land.*
*What a day, glorious day, that will be.*

—MILLARD POSTHUMA

# HOW BEAUTIFUL HEAVEN MUST BE!

MRS. A. S. BRIDGEWATER, 1920

*We read of a place that's called Heaven,*
*It's made for the pure and the free;*
*These truths in God's Word He hath given,*
*How beautiful Heaven must be.*

*How beautiful Heaven must be,*
*Sweet home of the happy and free;*
*Fair haven of rest for the weary,*
*How beautiful Heaven must be.*

*In Heaven no drooping nor pining,*
*No wishing for elsewhere to be;*
*God's light is forever there shining,*
*How beautiful Heaven must be.*

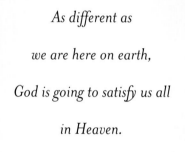

*As different as*

*we are here on earth,*

*God is going to satisfy us all*

*in Heaven.*

—GUY PENROD

# *What We Wonder*

lthough we have confidence in the Creator of Heaven, we're fuzzy on the details. We know all our hopes will be fulfilled in Heaven, but we don't know exactly how God is going to accomplish that. It's like having the travel brochure but no first—hand knowledge of the place we're going.

Among our main questions are:

What will Heaven be like?

What will we be like?

And what will it be like to live outside of time?

It's okay to ask such questions, as long as we understand that we won't have all the answers until we get there.

For the art of this book, we've tried to show Heaven as a glorified garden, a better—than—ever Eden, but all we really know is that it's better than we can imagine.

So, wonder with us for a while . . .

# What Will Heaven Be Like?

I love this Scripture: "The whole creation stands on tiptoe to see the wonderful light of the sons of God coming into their own. The world of creation cannot as yet see reality, not because it chooses to be blind, but because in God's purpose it has been so limited—yet it has been given hope. And the hope is that in the end the whole of created life will be rescued from the tyranny of change and decay, and will have its share in that magnificent liberty which can only belong to the children of God" (Romans 8:19–20, PHILLIPS). You see, the fall not only dragged down us as human beings and gave us disease, death, pain, tears, things that don't work, and joints that wear out, but it did the same thing to nature. But in Heaven nature will be liberated. We will see it released.

—GLORIA GAITHER

*Heaven goes by favor. If it went by merit,*
*you would stay out and your dog would go in.*

—MARK TWAIN

Heaven makes me think of the days when immigrants would come over to America. First the fathers would come to prepare a new home, and then they would send for the wife and kids. When the children got on the boat, all they had was Daddy's word, but they got on the boat and they came. That's what it's like for me: My big Brother and my Dad have a place ready for me and are going to bring me to it.

—RUSS TAFF

Sometimes we as Christians make Heaven sound somewhat boring—sitting around playing harps and floating around on clouds—when in reality it will be incredible. I leaned over to Russ Taff during a concert with twenty thousand people singing along and said, "Man, can you imagine what Heaven is going to be like, the rock that is going to take off there!" Picture the wildest, most musical concert you have been to and multiply it times one hundred, and at the same time magnify the most reverent moment you have been in. Things we enjoy on earth, we will enjoy perfected in Heaven, without the effects of sin and the fall.

—GUY PENROD

I think Heaven will be full of creatures. Maybe not a particular pet, I don't know. I just don't believe that God wastes anything that is good, especially if He went to so much trouble to create life on this earth with such incredible diversity and creativity.

—GLORIA GAITHER

# Heaven Will Be All of It

GLORIA GAITHER

Our children are grown now—in their early thirties. Two of them have families of their own. They all have creative vocations and are making a difference in ways that make Bill and me proud. If you would see these young adults, you would see them as they now are, and that would be good.

But when I see them, I see more than just this image of lovely young adults. I see the babies I held, the children who tumbled down our hillside in the fall leaves or winter snow. I see their first piano recitals and hear the new guitar licks. I see the poetry contests, the opening nights of the high school plays, the first recording projects of the band. I see fireworks on the Fourth of July, kids fishing in the creek and horseback riding at the 4–H fair. I see a young man presenting his animated video project, a young woman teaching a college English class, and a lovely lady hosting a reception for a theater cast. I see a bride, a new mother, a first homeowner. I see all this when one of our children walks down the stairs, under the grape arbor or through our kitchen door.

If you ask me to describe what Heaven will be, I think it will be "all of it." All the seasons—spring blossoms, summer fruit, fall harvest, winter rest—all going on simultaneously.

It will be the big picture, the full content. It will be the ultimate expansion of our gifts and abilities using everything we've ever learned with total freedom to create, think, enjoy, understand, and celebrate. Our loved ones will be beautiful beyond anything here, yet uniquely themselves in ways at which this life could only hint. All of the "perfect" will be there—of foods, sounds, sights, tastes, insights, experiences—and none of the ugly, negative, frustrating, or limiting. No sadness, no pain, no disappointment in ourselves or disillusionment with others. No lying, no deception, no crime.

Everything and everybody will have dimension. Heaven will be "all of it."

# BEAUTIFUL ISLE OF SOMEWHERE

### JESSIE B. POUNDS, 1897

*Somewhere the sun is shining,*
*Somewhere the songbirds dwell;*
*Hush, then, thy sad repining,*
*God lives, and all is well.*

*Somewhere, somewhere,*
*Beautiful Isle of Somewhere!*
*Land of the true, where we live anew,*
*Beautiful Isle of Somewhere!*

*Somewhere the load is lifted,*
*Close by an open door;*
*Somewhere the clouds are rifted,*
*Somewhere the angels sing.*

What will Heaven be like? I don't know, and I don't think anybody else does either. One Scripture says, "eye hath not seen, ear hath not heard, Neither has it entered into the heart of man what God has prepared for those that love Him" (1 Corinthians 2:9). This means that if you take Disney's imagination, and you mix it up with Beethoven's brilliance, and you wrap around Einstein's wildest dreams, then the best that those old boys could come up with would be a kindergarten play compared to what God has prepared for those who love Him. So I don't know what Heaven will be like, but I do know what we will be like because I remember another Scripture that says, "Beloved, now we are children of God, and it has not yet been revealed what we shall be, but we know that when He is revealed, we shall be like Him" (1 John 3:2). So what we will we be like? We will be like Jesus—33 and single.

—MARK LOWRY

Only two people know what Heaven is like—Adam and Eve. They are the only people who know about the Garden of Eden. The rest of us have to go on what we have heard, what it must be like. Here, you get about two weeks of life when everything is pretty cool and then something happens. Heaven to me is going to be a place where I am not hoping that something is going to happen. It is the place with no more tears and no more hurting, and a place where all my hopes are fulfilled. I no longer have to hope for anything. I simply exist in the presence of the Lord for an eternity.

—LARNELLE HARRIS

I think Heaven is a place where you are reunited with people you knew before they passed away. I think it is a wonderful place where angels are singing and the food is great and you are just happy.

—MADDIE ROSE TAFF (AGE 9)

I think Heaven's gonna' smell a lot like strawberries.

—LEE HAYES (AGE 7)

I remember Maddie Rose, our older daughter, asked me about a dog that got run over. She was standing there holding her little puppy, looking at me, and crying, "Why? Why?" Several months after the dog died she asked, "Daddy, will he be in Heaven?" Well, the Bible talks about the wolf dwelling with the lamb (Isaiah 11:6), so I said, "Honey, Heaven would not be complete if animals were not there. I know that you loved Rudy so much, and Jesus loves you so much, and He cried when Rudy died because you cried. I just think that your little dog will be waiting for you when you get there."

—RUSS TAFF

Heaven is that place of perfect peace. Life here is good, but stressful at times. Here we think of having a moment's peace; there peace is forever . . . and I want to go before my daughter starts dating.

—JONATHAN MARTIN

# JESUS, I HEARD YOU HAD A BIG HOUSE

### WILLIAM J. & GLORIA GAITHER, 1975

*Jesus, I heard You had a big house*
*Where I could have a room of my own*
*Jesus, I heard You had a big yard*
*Big enough to let a kid roam*
*I heard You had clothes in Your closet*
*Just the right size that I wear*
*And Jesus, I heard if I give You my heart*
*Then You'll let me go there*

*Jesus, I heard in Your big house*
*There's plenty of love to go around*
*I heard there's always singing and laughter*
*To fill the place with happy sounds*
*And I've been thinking that a Friend*
*Who planned to give me all that He's got*
*Before I'd even met Him*
*Well, He sure must love me a lot.*

*And Jesus I'd just like to tell You*
*Well, I sure do love you a lot.*

# I COULDN'T BEGIN TO TELL YOU

### ALBERT E. BRUMLEY, 1940

*If I had all the words of our language to use at a moment's command*
*If I had all the beautiful pictures of nature, the sea, and the land*
*If I spoke in a voice never ending, speaking only of loveliness*
*I couldn't begin to tell you how beautiful Heaven is.*

*If I mixed all the glorious sunsets with the fathomless mysteries of Mars*
*If I mixed all the beauty of spring time with the gleam of the moon and the stars*
*If I added the love of all mothers and the thrill of a baby's kiss*
*I couldn't, no I couldn't, begin to tell you how beautiful Heaven is.*

# The Glorious City

[9] Then one of the seven angels who had the seven bowls filled with the seven last plagues came to me and talked with me, saying, "Come, I will show you the bride, the Lamb's wife." [10] And he carried me away in the Spirit to a great and high mountain, and showed me the great city, the holy Jerusalem, descending out of heaven from God, [11] having the glory of God. Her light was like a most precious stone, like a jasper stone, clear as crystal. [12] Also she had a great and high wall with twelve gates, and twelve angels at the gates, and names written on them, which are the names of the twelve tribes of the children of Israel: . . . [14] Now the wall of the city had twelve foundations, and on them were the names of the twelve apostles of the Lamb. [15] And he who talked with me had a gold reed to measure the city, its gates, and its wall. [16] The city is laid out as a square; its length is as great as its breadth. And he measured the city with the reed: twelve thousand furlongs. Its length, breadth, and height are equal. [17] Then he measured its wall: one hundred and forty-four cubits, according to the measure of a man, that is, of an angel. [18] The construction of its wall was of jasper; and the city was pure gold, like clear glass. [19] The foundations of the wall of the city were adorned with all kinds of precious stones: . . .

<sup>21</sup>The twelve gates were twelve pearls: each individual gate was of one pearl. And the street of the city was pure gold, like transparent glass. <sup>22</sup> But I saw no temple in it, for the Lord God Almighty and the Lamb are its temple. <sup>23</sup>The city had no need of the sun or of the moon to shine in it, for the glory of God illuminated it. The Lamb is its light. <sup>24</sup>And the nations of those who are saved shall walk in its light, and the kings of the earth bring their glory and honor into it. <sup>25</sup>Its gates shall not be shut at all by day (there shall be no night there). <sup>26</sup>And they shall bring the glory and the honor of the nations into it. <sup>27</sup>But there shall by no means enter it anything that defiles, or causes an abomination or a lie, but only those who are written in the Lamb's Book of Life.

<sup>1</sup>And he showed me a pure river of water of life, clear as crystal, proceeding from the throne of God and of the Lamb. <sup>2</sup>In the middle of its street, and on either side of the river, was the tree of life, which bore twelve fruits, each tree yielding its fruit every month. The leaves of the tree were for the healing of the nations. <sup>3</sup>And there shall be no more curse, but the throne of God and of the Lamb shall be in it, and His servants shall serve Him. <sup>4</sup>They shall see His face, and His name shall be on their foreheads. <sup>5</sup>There shall be no night there: They need no lamp nor light of the sun, for the Lord God gives them light. And they shall reign forever and ever.

# What Will We Be Like?

*We are not merely human beings having a spiritual experience,*

*but rather spiritual beings having a human experience.*

—PIERRE TEILHARD DE CHARDIN

*Behold what manner of love the Father has bestowed on us, that we should be called children of God! Therefore the world does not know us, because it did not know Him. Beloved, now we are children of God; and it has not yet been revealed what we shall be, but we know that when He is revealed, we shall be like Him, for we shall see Him as He is. And everyone who has this hope in Him purifies himself, just as He is pure.*

—I JOHN 3:1–3

I wonder about the logistics of Heaven. Are we going to be the age at which we die? Are we going to know everybody there? Will we be married there or have children there? Will we grow our own food? What are we going to do? I mainly know we are going to worship Him.

—JANET PASCHAL

The Bible says that we do not know what we will be in Heaven, but we know that when we see Him we shall be like Him. (1 John 3:2) So what is like Him? Jesus the infant in Bethlehem, Jesus the crucified, Jesus the resurrected, Jesus the healer, Jesus the person who bears our iniquities and our sorrows? Yes. The Christ who laughed? Yes. All of that. The victorious King and Lord? Yes. When we see Him we shall be like Him.

Some of us say: I'm sad because we won't be husband and wife there, we won't be mother and daughter there. Trust me, the relationship that is coming will be so much more intense that we don't know how to explain it. It's like explaining to a child in the womb what it means to be married. Whatever relationships you have here, the relationships in Heaven will be much more intense than anything we've ever experienced.

—GLORIA GAITHER

I wonder whether people there know what we are doing here. Can they look down and see us? I wonder if my wife knows what we are going through here now?

—JAKE HESS

*When the dead rise, they will neither marry nor be given in marriage; they will be like the angels in Heaven.*

—MARK 12:25, NIV

Sad thoughts about earth—divorce, death, disease, or disability—those memories just won't happen in Heaven. Bad memories are going to be erased just like the stars are mitigated by the rising sun, because something so dazzling, so grand and glorious and brilliant and bright is going to happen up there that it's going to eclipse every dark memory. And we won't forget so much as we will have no more need to remember discouraging times.

—JONI EARECKSON TADA

*For our citizenship is in Heaven, from which we also eagerly wait for the Savior, the Lord Jesus Christ, who will transform our lowly body that it may be conformed to His glorious body, according to the working by which He is able even to subdue all things to Himself.*

—PHILIPPIANS 3:20–21

I am curious as to how emotions will work in Heaven. Except for glimpses, I've never known what it is like to feel completely clean in my soul and free from sin. We have those moments as believers where God does a number on us and cleans us out. The Holy Spirit is present, filling us and using us. You have a period of time maybe that you have gone where you have gotten victory over things, but then some sin creeps in and ruins the party. I think that whole idea that in Heaven there will not be any tears brought by sin is a real mystery.

—GUY PENROD

I wonder how we will know each other in Heaven. I have two little girls, and selfishly I hope I am always their daddy. I know we will all be one big family up there, but I wonder if I'll still have the structure of the love of my wife and my family.

—BUDDY MULLINS

My seminary professor Reinhold Neibuhr reminded us that the Bible has very little to say about the furniture of Heaven or the temperature of hell. What it does tell us very clearly is that it does not yet appear to us what we shall be, but we know that when we see Him we will be like Him because we will see Him face to face. The biblical hope isn't that we will be some kind of wispy invisible substance, but that we will like Jesus be resurrected bodies, recognizable and imperishable.

—DON COLLINS

Science keeps finding new planets, and they say there is an endless number of suns and each of those suns have a system. So when we talk about going up to Heaven, well, where is up anymore? It used to be simple, up was up. Heaven was on the other side of the moon. But now it is a big puzzle to me.

—CALVIN NEWTON

35 But someone will say, "How are the dead raised up? And with what body do they come?" 36 Foolish one, what you sow is not made alive unless it dies. 37 And what you sow, you do not sow that body that shall be, but mere grain—perhaps wheat or some other grain. 38 But God gives it a body as He pleases, and to each seed its own body.

. . . 42 So also is the resurrection of the dead. The body is sown in corruption, it is raised in incorruption. 43 It is sown in dishonor, it is raised in glory. It is sown in weakness, it is raised in power. 44 It is sown a natural body, it is raised a spiritual body. There is a natural body, and there is a spiritual body. 51 Behold, I tell you a mystery: We shall not all sleep, but we shall all be changed— 52 in a moment, in the twinkling of an eye, at the last trumpet. For the trumpet will sound, and the dead will be raised incorruptible, and we shall be changed. 53 For this corruptible must put on incorruption, and this mortal must put on immortality. 54 So when this corruptible has put on incorruption, and this mortal has put on immortality, then shall be brought to pass the saying that is written: "Death is swallowed up in victory."
55 "O Death, where is your sting?
O Hades, where is your victory?"
56 The sting of death is sin, and the strength of sin is the law. 57 But thanks be to God, who gives us the victory through our Lord Jesus Christ. 58 Therefore, my beloved brethren, be steadfast, immovable, always abounding in the work of the Lord, knowing that your labor is not in vain in the Lord.

—1 CORINTHIANS 15:35–58

# What Will Eternity Be Like?

I don't believe eternity starts out there some place; eternity starts here. It starts the moment we turn our lives over to Christ. And the promise to believers is that nothing will interrupt that eternal perspective.

— GLORIA GAITHER

"Of old You laid the foundation of the earth,
And the heavens are the work of Your hands.
They will perish, but You will endure;
Yes, they will all grow old like a garment;
Like a cloak You will change them,
And they will be changed.
But You are the same,
And Your years will have no end.
The children of Your servants will continue,
And their descendants will be established before You."

— PSALM 102: 25–28

*I believe that in the life to come, I shall have the senses*
*I have not had here, and that my home there will be beautiful with*
*color, music and with the speech of flowers and the faces I love.*

—HELEN KELLER

I believe in the eternal now. I think one of the greatest theological things ever to happen is Einstein's theory of relativity, because he discovered that at the speed of light time stands still. It is only now. Christ said over, and over, and over again, "I am light." "I am light." In light, God is. So in that perspective the crucifixion, the resurrection, the second coming, the creation of Eden are all present tense. We can't understand that, but at the speed of light is eternal now; Heaven is now. And it is forever!

—GLORIA GAITHER

In Ecclesiastes it says "God has put eternity in the hearts on men" (Eccesiastes 3:11). We were created for eternity, but we're so comfortable with this life that it's hard to move to the unknown. It's like staying in an abusive situation—it's what you know.

—BILLY BLACKWOOD

It's hard to imagine a place where time is of no value. Time is such an enemy here now that I can't imagine what it is going to be like to not have to be concerned about how long stuff is going to take. I am longing for that.

—BUDDY GREENE

# WHERE WE'LL NEVER GROW OLD

### JAMES CLEVELAND MOORE, 1914

*I have heard of a land on the far away strand,*
*'Tis a beautiful home of the soul;*
*Built by Jesus on high, where we never shall die,*
*'Tis a land where we never grow old.*

*Never grow old, never grow old,*
*In a land where we'll never grow old;*
*Never grow old, never grow old,*
*In a land where we'll never grow old.*

*In that beautiful home where we'll never more roam,*
*We shall be in the sweet by and by;*
*Happy praise to the King through eternity sing,*
*'Tis a land where we never shall die.*

The ending of *The Last Battle*, book 7 of the Chronicles of Narnia, by C. S. Lewis:

> And for us this is the end of all the stories and we can most truly say that they all lived happily ever after. But for them, it was only the beginning of the real story. All their life in this world and all the adventures in Narnia had only been the cover and the title page. Now at last they were beginning Chapter I of the great story which no one on earth has read, which goes on forever, in which every chapter is better than the one before.

We are told that our worship of God will be eternal and in ever—increasing measures of joy, and I find that just stymieing. It is so difficult to absorb. In the book of Isaiah (6:3) where it is described that the seraphim continually call out before God the Father day and night, "Holy, Holy, Holy, Lord God Almighty, Heaven and earth are full of thy glory. Holy, Holy, Holy," they say day and night, and night and day. They have been doing that for millennia and will continue to do that for millennia more. To me that is like singing the same chorus in church 579 times, 579 Sundays in a row. So what's mysterious to me is how this ever—increasing capacity for worship will constantly remain fresh and constantly remain new. I once heard someone say it's like maybe God, when He reveals some attribute of Himself to the seraphim, they all say, "Holy, Holy, Holy." Then when they cover with their wings to contemplate it, He turns and another attribute is revealed, and they look up and say, "Oh, I didn't know that about You." So they say, "Holy, Holy, Holy" again. If we going to be constantly discovering something fresh and new about God—and that He has the capacity to be full of that infinite variety—it is just mind blowing. I think that is the biggest mystery to me: to keep getting younger, and keep getting wiser, and to keep having your heart stretched more for worship.

—JONI EARECKSON TADA

*And this is eternal life, that they may know You, the only true God, and Jesus Christ whom You have sent*

—JOHN 17:3

"Let not your heart be troubled; you
believe in God, believe also in Me.
In My Father's house are many
mansions; if it were not so, I would have
told you. I go to prepare a place for you.
And if I go and prepare a place for you,
I will come again and receive you to
Myself; that where I am, there you may
be also. And where I go you know, and
the way you know." . . . "I am the way,
the truth, and the life. No one comes to
the Father except through Me."

—JESUS OF NAZARETH
(John 14:1–6)

# What We Know

ost details about Heaven we just have to wonder for now, but we can stake everything on three things that we do know:

Jesus is there, preparing it for us.

We get to live there forever.

It's going to be more wonderful than we can possibly imagine.

Be confident in Heaven. Believe in it.

Jesus has promised, and He always keeps His Word.

# It's Our Home Forever

A Catholic priest friend of mine says, "Christianity promises you two things; that your life will have meaning and that you will live forever. And if you get a better offer, you should take it."

— BECCA STEVENS

*For God so loved the world that He gave His only begotten Son, that whoever believes in Him should not perish but have everlasting life.*

— JOHN 3 : 16

It astounds me to think that Jesus is preparing a place for me. Some people say there is going to be nothing but mansions, but I don't care what's there. I don't care about streets of gold, a dusty trail would be fine. All I want to do is be with Jesus and the people who love Him and love each other. I really don't care, as long as I have my loved ones and my dogs, and everyone is safe to love and be free.

— CALVIN NEWTON

*Heaven will not be filled with sorrow.*

*No diseased or crippled bodies. No Tempter,*

*as Satan will be cast into the bottomless pit.*

*Neither will there be any darkness,*

*for the Lamb is the light.*

*What a wonderful place to spend eternity*

*being with our Lord and Savior.*

—LILLIE KNAULS

# Jesus Is There, Preparing Heaven

*And He said to him, "Most assuredly, I say to you, hereafter you shall see Heaven open, and the angels of God ascending and descending upon the Son of Man."*

—JOHN 1:51

I am looking forward to seeing what Jesus really looks like. You can imagine all day long. You can dream about it, write about it, and sing about it, but to actually see Heaven materialize right before my very eyes will be more than words can describe.

—BABBIE MASON

Jesus knows what I love, so I think He is preparing me a beach house.

—GLORIA GAITHER

If God can make the earth in six days, Heaven has got to be wonderful. Jesus has been up there almost two thousand years preparing it.

—DAVID RING

Jesus is the God who can speak anything into existence, and He also was a carpenter here on earth. He has gone back to prepare a place for us. Maybe it sounds humorous, but I can imagine Him preparing Heaven physically, because He loves us so much, and individually, because He wants all of us to have His personal touch.

—BUDDY MULLINS

*He is the image of the invisible God, the firstborn over all creation. For by Him all things were created that are in heaven and that are on earth, visible and invisible, whether thrones or dominions or principalities or powers. All things were created through Him and for Him. And He is before all things, and in Him all things consist. And He is the head of the body, the church, who is the beginning, the firstborn from the dead, that in all things He may have the preeminence. For it pleased the Father that in Him all the fullness should dwell, and by Him to reconcile all things to Himself, by Him, whether things on earth or things in Heaven, having made peace through the blood of His cross.*

—COLOSSIANS 1:15–20

# Next Time We Meet

GLORIA GAITHER

Ever since the Israelites were dispersed by a long parade of captors to the far corners of the globe, Jewish families would lift their cups of wine at the end of the Sedar supper and say "Next year in Jerusalem!" This phrase kept alive the hope that one day the great family of Abraham's descendants would gather in the Holy City free from all bondage and suffering and there celebrate the ultimate deliverance promised so long ago.

Centuries of conflict and cruelty certainly would have dimmed that hope. For as long as the weak are crushed by the strong, the dream of a utopia on earth seems more and more unlikely. Were it not for a glorious, "big picture revelation" given to the disciple Jesus loved so much, at the ebbing moments of John's earthly existence. Here are his words as he struggled to express what God was showing him:

"I saw a holy Jerusalem, new-created, descending resplendent out of Heaven, as ready for God as a bride for her husband. I heard a voice thunder from the Throne, 'Look! Look! God has moved into the neighborhood making His home with men and women! They are His people. He is their God. He'll wipe every tear from their eyes. Death is gone for good—tears gone, crying gone, pain gone—all the first order of things gone.' The Enthroned continued, "Look! I am making everything new. Write it all down—each word dependable and accurate."

Then He said, "It's happened. I am A to Z. I am the Beginning, I am the Conclusion. From Water–of–Life Well I give freely to the thirsty. Conquerors inherit all this. I'll be God to them, they'll be sons and daughters to Me" (Revelation 21:2–7, THE MESSAGE).

So listen, children, believe it. Raise your cups of joy. It is certain . . . next year in Jerusalem.

# It's Going to Be Wonderful

Heaven is too wonderful for words. I can't describe it. It would be like asking a caterpillar about flying, like asking a flower bulb what is like to be fragrant, or like asking a coconut, all hard and hairy, what it is like to be swaying in the breeze and be all tall and beautiful. A coconut can't imagine that. A caterpillar can't imagine flying. A bulb can't ever imagine what it is to be fragrant. A peach pit has no concept what it means to bear fruit and give shade and be delightful. And yet within each of those little things is that seed, that identity, of what one day it will become, of what one day it is destined to be. Somewhere within me is this seed of what one day I am destined to be. What I will be then is who I am now. The pattern of it is somehow within me, but I cannot even begin to imagine it. I have just got a coconut brain, like a flower bulb trying to think fragrance.

—JONI EARECKSON TADA

Heaven is not just a place; it's a state of being that's so fulfilling that we can't describe it.

—BILLY BLACKWOOD

*And the Spirit and the bride say, "Come!" And let him who hears say, "Come!" And let him who thirsts come. Whoever desires, let him take the water of life freely.*

— REVELATION 22:17

Here, I think we might be able to experience only tiny bits of Heaven, because we are too constrained by our bodies and minds. There is a completely different set of rules, and all the things that have formed us into the people who we are now will not necessarily rule who we are over there. We will have different bodies, and we will not be governed by the guilt of the past or the sins of the future.

— DAVID PHELPS

Heaven is impossible to put into words because Scripture only gives us a taste or a peek. It is just too big! Our wildest imagination can't even begin to capture it. Scripture says that He is able to do much more than we can ask, or think, or imagine, I think that is the way we have to look at Heaven.

— EVIE KARLSSON

Most people I know say that they could care less about all the fancy stuff Heaven has to offer. Well, not me. I really like the idea of all that fancy stuff. I can just picture me in my big ol' crown. I can picture those gates made of humongous pearls, and streets so bright you have to put on your movie star size glasses before you take a walk. And I can see myself walking up and down those streets of gold talking to all my friends—the very same friends who said they didn't care about all the fancy stuff. Heaven is a real place, a place to look forward to, to contemplate, to prepare for. The beauty of it will be beyond our imaginations. Those we've loved and long to see will be there, and all we could desire or hope for will be provided. And we will be with our Lord. Sounds like a party to me. Strike up the band!

—SUE BUCHANAN

*The saints of the Most High shall receive the kingdom, and possess the kingdom forever, even forever and ever.*

—DANIEL 7:18

Heaven is a city whose Builder and Maker is God, and it is more real than this city where I live today. Heaven is all that the loving heart of God desires, the limitless mind of God can conceive, and the lavish hand of God can create.

—ADRIAN ROGERS

I live alone. Breakfast is finished, I'm sitting in my favorite chair by the fire with my dog, Fritz, at my feet. I have my leather jacket thrown over my knees, giving him a clear signal that we are going somewhere, hopefully not to the vet or to the kennels. I talk a lot to Fritz, and he's a good listener, cocking his ears, wagging his tail, intent on my every word. Telling him that we're going out in the country to a farm. There will be no restraining leash, there will be rabbits and squirrels to chase and other dogs to romp with. He's listening as I describe in detail the wonders he's about to enjoy. Alas, he really does not understand a single thing I am saying, but he is full of hope and excitement as we rise and head for the door. I'm now 83, well beyond the average life expectancy, in the last chapter of my life. My thoughts turn on occasion to Heaven, but I find only symbols and earthly vocabulary to think with. Here Fritz and I have the same problem. Thankfully, the Word of the Master assures me that there is nothing to fear, that Heaven will be my home, and my God of love, light, joy, and unimaginable possibilities will meet me there.

—ROBERT REARDON

VEN

*Here
and Now*

"Do not lay up for yourselves treasures on earth, where moth and rust destroy and where thieves break in and steal; but lay up for yourselves treasures in Heaven, where neither moth nor rust destroys and where thieves do not break in and steal. For where your treasure is, there your heart will be also."

—Jesus of Nazareth
(*Matthew 6:19–21*)

# It Affects How We Live

I f Heaven is the home of all our hopes, then that hope must influence how we live and how we die here on earth.

Everything about our lives can be viewed from a higher, eternal perspective. Our relationships truly have the potential to last forever.

We have something wonderful beyond words to celebrate in the ways we worship and in the ways we live, and we have an urgent message of hope and wholeness to share with our children and with our neighbors.

Heaven isn't just for tomorrow—it's for right now!

# I THEN SHALL LIVE

GLORIA GAITHER, 1981

To the tune of Finlandia

*I then shall live as one who's been forgiven;*
*I'll walk with joy to know my debts are paid.*
*I know my name is clear before my Father;*
*I am His child, and I am not afraid.*
*So greatly pardoned, I'll forgive my brother;*
*The law of love I gladly will obey.*

*I then shall live as one who's learned compassion;*
*I've been so loved that I'll risk loving, too.*
*I know how fear builds walls instead of bridges;*
*I dare to see another's point of view.*
*And when relationships demand commitment,*
*Then I'll be there to care and follow through.*

*Your Kingdom come around and through and in me,*
*Your pow'r and glory, let them shine though me;*
*Your Hallowed Name, O may I bear with honor,*
*And may Your living Kingdom come in me.*
*The Bread of Life, may I share with honor,*
*And may You feed a hungry world through me.*

# We Have An Eternal Perspective

Recognize the eternal in the moment. There is a lot of difference between minutes and moments, and I think the whole purpose of human life as we know it is to find what is eternal, and give ourselves away to things that last forever. We must make moments, not just take up minutes.

What are the two things that survive this world? Relationships with people and relationship with God and His Word. Everything else is going to go. So what was Jesus saying when He said, "Lay up for yourselves treasures in Heaven?" (Matthew 6:20) Invest in the two things that survive this world, because everything else goes. We have to make a living, that's earth stuff. The ultimate use of my time, the reason I say "yes" to this and "no" to that, on a daily basis must be more and more eternal. I ask, "Is there eternity in it?" If there is no eternity in it, why do it?

—GLORIA GAITHER

There's a wonderful Old Testament verse: "The stones that were fit for the Temple were all dressed in the quarry. There was not a sound of chisel or hammer at the site of the temple" (1 Kings 6:7). Down here on earth is all the chiseling and the hammering and the honing and the shaping and the refining and the polishing. But our sufferings fit us to be jewels in His crown, and I can't wait.

—JONI EARECKSON TADA

*This is a faithful saying:*
*For if we died with Him,*
*We shall also live with Him.*
*If we endure,*
*We shall also reign with Him.*
*If we deny Him,*
*He also will deny us.*
*If we are faithless,*
*He remains faithful;*
*He cannot deny Himself.*

—2 TIMOTHY 2:11–13

I hope that if anyone has not made a decision to give their heart and soul to Jesus and happens to get a hold of this video and this book, that they will see the reality of Heaven, that they will make a decision to humble themselves before God.

—GUY PENROD

# BECAUSE HE LIVES

## WILLIAM J. & GLORIA GAITHER, 1971

*God sent His Son, they called Him Jesus,*
*He came to love, heal, and forgive;*
*He lived and died to buy my pardon,*
*An empty grave is there to prove my Savior lives.*

*Because He lives I face tomorrow,*
*Because He lives all fear is gone;*
*Because I know He holds the future,*
*And life is worth the living just because He lives.*

*And then one day I'll cross the river,*
*I'll fight life's final war with pain;*
*And then as death gives way to victory,*
*I'll see the lights of glory and I'll know He lives.*

## IT'S NOT ABOUT NOW
### GLORIA GAITHER, 2001

*They'd only had such a short little while*
*To love and to heal and to learn how to smile*
*It didn't seem fair when she had to let go*
*To let him slip from her arms when she needed him so.*

*It's not about now*
*It's not about here*
*It's all about then when there's nothing to fear*
*It's all about then, there—the mystery's clear*
*When then will be now*
*and there will be here.*

While I always believed in Heaven and knew it was there, it wasn't until my dad went on ahead of me that I realized several notches deeper what we have to look forward to. His passing does nothing but reinforce for me the reality that Heaven holds. I have no fear at all, even with everything that has been going on since the terrorist attacks. I am living in this understanding that whether I live or die, I belong to the Lord. When we get into a car and drive the highway or get into an airplane or go to a doctor, who knows what we are going to experience, who knows if this is our last day? It could be today that the Lord comes to take us home or that we go through the corridor of death into life forever.

—EVIE KARLSSON

*And the Lord will deliver me from every evil work and preserve me for His heavenly kingdom. To Him be glory forever and ever. Amen!*

—2 TIMOTHY 4:18

Why is Heaven so important? Because hell is important and you don't want to go there. It is forever, and there is life after death according to the Bible. Where we are going to spend it is a big deal. The Lord has been showing me how things matter on an eternal basis. Everything that we do here, eventually we are going to answer for it.

—SARAH DELANE

I experience Heaven on earth on a daily basis in prayer and communion with Him, in the love of my family, my husband, my children, my friends. When we get together for these Gaither Homecomings, I think it is a little slice of Heaven. And understanding that as wonderful as the best times here on earth can be, it just does not scratch the surface.

—EVIE KARLSSON

*Remember that in a race everyone runs, but only one person gets the prize. You also must run in such a way that you will win. All athletes practice strict self-control. They do it to win a prize that will fade away, but we do it for an eternal prize. So I run straight to the goal with purpose in every step.*

—I CORINTHIANS 9:24–26, NLT

I think of Heaven like being on earth with all of the impurities removed. Everything is perfect there. My wife is there. I have eleven brothers and sisters, my mother and dad all there. So Heaven has just got to be that perfect earth.

—JAKE HESS

Why wouldn't you want to know Someone who loves you that much? To think that God, Creator of the universe, who doesn't need anything, desires YOU.

—BILLY BLACKWOOD

Can we experience Heaven on earth? Yes, and I think we have it on pretty good authority. Christ Himself said the Kingdom of Heaven has already come (Matthew 4:17). The Kingdom is among you, and it is within you. It is all around you. There are these moments that we have where we can glimpse some sense of what the Kingdom to come is like, like a transcending moment. I think that is the reason that Christ came—so we would have some sense of what is to come and so that we could, in fact, experience that Kingdom on earth. It is not a question of *can* we experience Heaven on earth; it is a question of whether or not we *will* do it.

—ROBERT BENSON


I believed in hell long before I believed in Heaven. In fact, I believed in hell before I believed there was a God. The news to me was Heaven. Like so many people I couldn't forgive myself for my failures. And if I couldn't forgive myself, how could Jesus Christ forgive me? Until I finally understood that forgiveness is His business. If you're still dwelling on past sins that Christ has forgiven, you might have serious questions about going to Heaven. Only if you've been forgiven by Christ do you go to Heaven. Having that forgiveness is a wonderful relief and a terrific assurance. It changes your marriage. It changes your family. It changes your work. It changes your life.

—BEN HAYDEN

If you read history you will find that the Christians who did most for the present world were those who thought most of the next. The apostles themselves, who laid the foundation for the conversion of the Roman Empire, the great men who built up the Middle Ages, the English evangelicals who abolished the slave trade—all left their mark on earth precisely because their minds were occupied with Heaven.

—C.S. LEWIS

I think the bottom line is that Heaven is our hope. When we set out on our life's journey, Heaven is the direction we are headed, our desired goal. We are going to have trials here. God never promised everything would be the way we think it should be, but He did say that one day we wouldn't weep anymore, and we wouldn't feel the losses that we feel and the struggle. Here we should embrace life as we know it, and make the most of every day, and be the very best of whatever we strive to be. Work hard, and find every ounce of good and every ounce of ability that you have within yourself. But understand that this is all temporary. This is not the final chapter—don't compromise eternal things for temporary things.

—JANET PASCHAL

*Fight the good fight of faith, lay hold on eternal life, to which you were also called and have confessed the good confession in the presence of many witnesses.*

—1 TIMOTHY 6:12

*Aim at Heaven*

*and you will get*

*earth thrown in;*

*aim at earth and*

*you will get neither.*

—C. S. LEWIS

Too often here on earth we walk by sight and not by faith. Material stuff is truly a distraction, but when you stop to realize some things—that my car is going to wear out, my plumbing is going to eventually back up, I am going to gain weight and lose my hair, my husband is going to get a middle, and all the stuff that we work so hard to maintain is going to let us down—you realize that it is just stuff. Last night our oldest son's car was stolen. When you realize possessions are like water going through your hands, you just thank God you have insurance and keep going. And you hold these things very loosely. On the other hand, we are expecting our first grandchild, and relationships are the things you hold onto for dear life. You have the joy and the responsibility to pass on those things that really matter. And it is not a Chevy Blazer; it is the heritage of my faith that I inherited. Focus on the treasures of Heaven, not the stuff of earth.

—BABBIE MASON

*Do not love the world or the things in the world. If anyone loves the world, the love of the Father is not in him. For all that is in the world—the lust of the flesh, the lust of the eyes, and the pride of life—is not of the Father but is of the world. And the world is passing away, and the lust of it; but he who does the will of God abides forever.*

—1 JOHN 2:15–17

All of the things that are important to us here, I can't imagine that they will be important there. We live now in a place that is driven by how much we can do and how much we can accumulate. If you have your eyes set on Heaven, then you need to turn your mind away from those things. But it is hard. It is hard to keep living like an alien in this world, but that is really it. We are made for Heaven.

— DAVID PHELPS

When you lose someone you go through a whole circle of faith. You cling desperately to the hope of Heaven and you have to believe in it again. You go through, "Is Heaven real? Because it better be real, because those people that I love are there, and God, You'd better keep Your promise!" God brings you around that circle, and Heaven means more, and is deeper and greater to you each time you lose someone. You come to the epiphany each time, "Hey, Heaven is real!" I have been through death a lot in my lifetime. My sister died when I was 15. Then my aunts and two uncles died right before my Mom. Every death is different, and everyone deals with grief differently. Some people don't want to talk about it, and some people want to smile. But you will deal with it eventually. I put off dealing with my sister's death for six years, but with my Mom, I wanted to feel every bit of grief. I felt everything I could feel with it, total grief, everything. I traveled the full circle of grief and then colored it in.

— LADYE LOVE SMITH

There are times when certain passages of Scripture that you have known all your life suddenly become almost like life bread to you. In Paul's second letter to the church in Corinth, he said, "You know all we are in our best moments, we are just earthen vessels" (2 Corinthians 4:7). Now saying that to people in Corinth, which was a big shipping port where everything was carried around in an earthen vessel, would be like saying to people in Chicago, "You know what, we are just the cardboard boxes." And reading that gave me a fresh insight into what our life is, we are a cardboard box to hold this treasure which is the life of Jesus Christ. I saw that really powerfully last year. My father-in-law, William, lived with us for two years. He was eighty years old, a wonderful man. Last Christmas my son, Christian, and I were home with William, and he went upstairs to take a bath, and Christian got ready for bed and was waiting to kiss his Papa goodnight. When William didn't come down for awhile, I went upstairs and knocked on the door. No answer. I knocked again, and I opened the door and there was William lying on the floor with his head in a pool of blood. He was still conscious,

and I knelt beside him and said, "Papa are you okay?" And he said, "I don't know." And I realized how blue his lips were, and even as I am calling 9-1-1 I realized that my four–year-old son was standing at the bathroom door watching. And Christian said, "Mommy what's wrong with Papa?" And I said, "Papa doesn't feel very good darling, but we are going to get some help." And he said, "Well, could I help?" And I said, "Yes, why don't you get a washrag and wipe Papa's forehead." So he did that. Only ten minutes left. You never know when you only have ten minutes left. When Christian and I got to the hospital, we followed the ambulance, and a very sweet doctor told me there was nothing that they could do. And I asked, "Can I see him?" A nurse took care of Christian as I walked down the corridor, and I opened the door to where this darling man who had been like a father to me was lying, so still with a sheet up to his neck. I saw in that moment that all that was left was the cardboard box, that William was home free. And I realized that it took some of the fear of death away from me because I understood all that was left was a shell and the treasure was home.

—SHEILA WALSH

*But we have this treasure in jars of clay to show that this all-surpassing power is from God and not from us.*

2 CORINTHIANS 4:7

Have you ever had a wonderful nightmare? I know those two words don't go together, but it's the only way I know to describe what life is very often like. For instance, my husband, Nathan, has endured many serious medical problems—it's been nightmarish in many, many ways. But there is also the other side to it—the wonderfulness. The wonderfulness is the awareness that God is faithful and the awareness of His presence in all circumstances. There is that wonderful feeling as we celebrate each day that God gives us together. There is the love and support of family and friends. Both the nightmare and the wonderfulness are real. And when I think about Heaven and wonder about Heaven will be like, it seems to me that the nightmare will all be gone and all we will have left is just the wonderfulness. And as wonderful as it is in this life now, with God's presence and His faithfulness I know that is just a pale image to what it will be like when we really see Him face to face.

—ANN SMITH

If we lose sight of a perspective about Heaven, then when troubles and trials and challenges come, I'm not sure we'll really keep the faith. We get so discouraged we want to give up and quit The old hymn writers really knew that if we lose sight of Heaven and we forget that Heaven is a place prepared for us, then it's really hard to make it through day by day.

—ROB MEHL

# HOLD TO GOD'S
# UNCHANGING HAND

JENNIE WILSON, 1904

*Time is filled with swift transition—*
*Naught of earth unmoved can stand—*
*Build your hopes on things eternal,*
*Hold to God's unchanging hand.*

*When your journey is completed,*
*If to God you have been true,*
*Fair and bright the home in glory*
*Your enraptured soul shall view.*

# CANAANLAND
# IS JUST IN SIGHT

JEFF GIBSON, 1983

*Though we walk through valleys*
*Though we climb high mountains*
*We must not give up the fight.*
*We must be like Moses*
*We've got to keep on going.*
*Canaanland is just in sight.*

*There will be no sorrow*
*There in that tomorrow*
*We will be there by and by.*
*Milk and honey flowing*
*That is where I'm going*
*Canaanland is just in sight*

# We Have Eternal Relationships

When you have lost a child, a young son or daughter, or a wife of sixty summers, your mind is inevitably drawn to thoughts of Heaven and the mystery of the afterlife. When my father died suddenly, Mother carried her grief and loneliness with Christian grace. But she never talked to me about Heaven or speculated about what life was like beyond the grave. She carried the unshakable assurance that Dad was with God. However, she found a secret in her grief for those who are left behind. I have found it to be a fundamental truth. She said you should give away what it is that you need the most. Then healing, joy, and the fulfillment of your own need would follow.

—ROBERT REARDON

There are so many people in Heaven whom I love, and it is so good to think they know each other now! It makes Heaven more real and more valuable to me.

—LADYE LOVE SMITH

*But I do not want you to be ignorant, brethren, concerning those who have fallen asleep, lest you sorrow as others who have no hope. For if we believe that Jesus died and rose again, even so God will bring with Him those who sleep in Jesus.*

*For this we say to you by the word of the Lord, that we who are alive and remain until the coming of the Lord will by no means precede those who are asleep. For the Lord Himself will descend from heaven with a shout, with the voice of an archangel, and with the trumpet of God. And the dead in Christ will rise first. Then we who are alive and remain shall be caught up together with them in the clouds to meet the Lord in the air. And thus we shall always be with the Lord. Therefore comfort one another with these words.*

—1 THESSALONIANS 4:13–18

Here on earth, I experience bits of Heaven with my family, with my girls, and with my wife. Heaven is relationships. Heaven is a relationship with Jesus. For too long I sang and performed about having that relationship with Christ but didn't have the real relationship that I am learning to enjoy now. I can experience Heaven when everybody is in bed and I am having time with the Lord—just a moment or glimpse of Him sitting right here with me. He really cares about what I am going through. That is Heaven to me.

—BUDDY MULLINS

HEAVEN

# WHAT ARE THEY DOING IN HEAVEN?

### CHARLES ALBERT TINDLE, 1901

*I'm thinking of friends who I used to know*
*Who lived and suffered in this world below*
*They've gone up to Heaven and I want to know*
*I wonder what are they doing there now.*

*I wonder what are they doing up in Heaven today*
*Where sins and sorrow are all gone away*
*Where peace abounds like a river, they say*
*I wonder what are they doing there now*

*There were some whose bodies were full of disease*
*No medicine and no doctor could give them much ease*
*They suffered until death would bring them sweet release*
*I wonder what are they doing there now.*

# We Have Something to Celebrate

*"As the Father loved Me, I also have loved you; abide in My love. If you keep My commandments, you will abide in My love, just as I have kept My Father's commandments and abide in His love. These things I have spoken to you, that My joy may remain in you, and that your joy may be full."*

JOHN 15:9-11

Heaven becomes more real at the funerals of saints. One I will speak about is a man who moved to Franklin, Tennessee, knowing that he was going to die within a few years, and he just set about involving himself in the community. He was an agent of reconciliation mainly between African–Americans and whites, and he started with ministers and pastors. When he finally died it was just the most remarkable testimony when his coffin was carried in by this multi–racial group of men who loved him. It was just so powerful to see what happens when a man loves the way Jesus loves and gets excited about the things that excite Jesus. It changes lives. So to me that day we got a glimpse of Heaven. It was just incredible.

— BUDDY GREENE

When we get bogged down in the world we're like a fellow who saved all his money to buy a passage on the Queen Mary. He bought a ticket, and he bought enough cheese and crackers for three weeks to get him through the trip. Every mealtime he would sit outside the restaurant and eat his cheese and crackers. One day the chef walked up to him and said, "Sir, I can prepare anything for you, just name it." The passenger got really embarrassed and said, "Well, all I had was enough money for my ticket, and I bought these cheese and crackers just to get me to America." Then the chef replied, "Didn't anyone tell you the meals were included in the ticket?" I often think that is the way we live. We have the words of Jesus that have the power to change circumstances. He said, "I will take care of you, I will supply your need." But, I think so many times we sit and eat our cheese and crackers and never really move into the place where He says, "Come on in and have a meal, I will take care of it for you."

—RUSS TAFF

Knowing the hope we have that we will live again makes us want to live this lifetime covered with words about the beauty of Jesus Christ. Because of Him we will all live again.

—SHEILA WALSH

When we receive Christ, Heaven has already begun in our soul. We have a piece of Him already inside of us. Eternity should be a daily thing. God has started it in me now and will continue it forever.

—SARAH DELANE

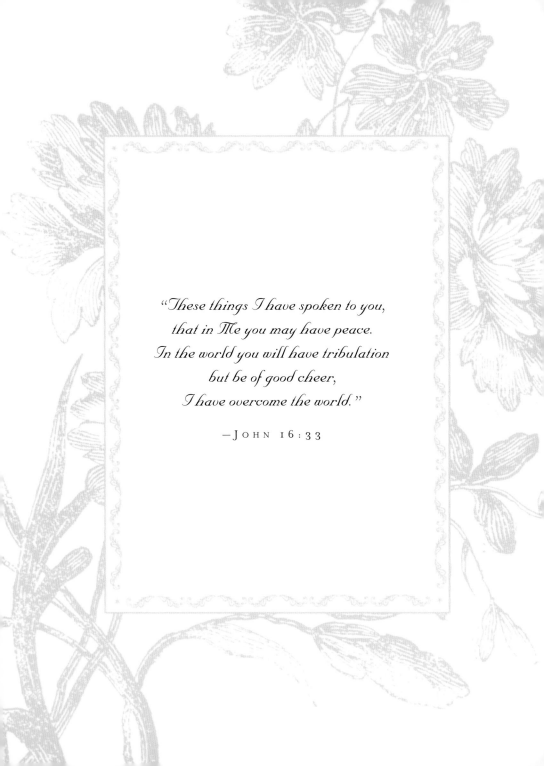

"These things I have spoken to you,
that in Me you may have peace.
In the world you will have tribulation
but be of good cheer,
I have overcome the world."

—JOHN 16:33

# We Have Something to Share

*For we are to God the fragrance of Christ among those who are being saved and among those who are perishing.*

— 2 CORINTHIANS 2:15

Prior to September 11, 2001, we lived in a culture where we didn't want to embrace the concepts of Christianity because they relate so much to being a servant—we would rather be served than to serve. But since then we have been forced to look our mortality in the face. More and more people are open to those questions of "who am I," "why am I here," and "where am I going after I die?" More and more people are open to the message of the gospel and they want that security, that family, and those church relationships. People want to know they lived with meaning and purpose, and they are exploring all the things that have to do with eternity. This is the challenge to us as believers to step up to the spiritual plate, so to speak, and minister to our friends, our family, our loved ones, and take advantage of those moments to talk about Heaven.

— BABBIE MASON

I remember when I thought that singing about Heaven was some form of escapism, that if I really wanted to be any good in this world, I would just work hard to make it a better place. Trouble was that most of the time I didn't. But as I began to see my own need for forgiveness and hear the good news, that because of the good work of Jesus on my behalf, I am forever loved by God and completely forgiven. Then the stuff that Jesus talked about—loving our enemies, helping our neighbors, serving the poor, being reconciled to God and my fellow man—all this stuff about His Kingdom began to produce a real longing in me. Slowly but surely, I began to pray with Jesus to our Heavenly Father, "Thy Kingdom come, thy will be done on earth as it is in Heaven" (Matthew 6:10).

—BUDDY GREENE

*"Also I say to you, whoever confesses Me before men, him the Son of Man also will confess before the angels of God. But he who denies Me before men will be denied before the angels of God."*

—LUKE 12:8–9

You are a Christian because someone whom you respected said something. They were in step with you some way. They didn't grab you and make you choose Christ. I tell people that if you respect what I do and who I am, if you respect my relationship with you here, then know that the best is yet to come. Eternity is the most important question of mankind.

—LARNELLE HARRIS

*Blessed be the God and Father of our Lord Jesus Christ, the Father of mercies and God of all comfort, who comforts us in all our tribulation, that we may be able to comfort those who are in any trouble, with the comfort with which we ourselves are comforted by God.*

— 2 CORINTHIANS 1 : 3 — 4

Tragedies like September 11 just shake the foundation of every person who sees the event. I think what encourages me is that such shock proves that God created each of us with a hole that can only be filled by Him. Whenever we are really put against the wall, what comes out is this incredible desire to believe that there is a God and there is a Heaven somewhere. I think it is very important to our whole life and culture to believe that there is a Heaven. Whenever something like September 11 happens, you just have to hold onto the faith that this earth is not the end.

— BUDDY MULLINS

I remember a widow preaching the gospel at her husband's funeral: "Friends, Charlie loves you and he wants to see you all in Heaven, but if you put your faith in the things of this world you are just going to miss it." And everybody was just in awe. I was standing right beside her, and reached over and touched her on her shoulder to comfort her. Her eyes were filled with tears, but she was just beaming. She knew that of the one hundred or so people gathered at the graveside service, that maybe half of them were trusting the world and not the Savior. God just raised her up at that moment.

— BUDDY GREENE

Sometimes our collective preoccupation with the Kingdom that is to come makes it really difficult to see the Kingdom that has already come. Thereby, it makes it even more difficult to participate in the delivery of the Kingdom that has already come, because we have a tendency to operate as though we are only passing through on the way to the real Kingdom. And the Kingdom that is here is just as real as the Kingdom that is there. I worry sometimes about us thinking so much about that life that we miss this one.

—ROBERT BENSON

*And He said to them, "Go into all the world and preach the gospel to every creature. He who believes and is baptized will be saved; but he who does not believe will be condemned."*

—MARK 16:15–16

When my daddy passed away, my children were young. And when they saw their grandfather lying in the casket and they were trying to put all of those pieces together, I explained to them like this: "The real Grandpa is in Heaven with Jesus and right here is just an empty cardboard box. This is just a shell. One day we are going to have this great big family reunion like we have every summer with all of your uncles and aunts and all the people that you love." The thing that I hang onto now is the great heritage of growing up in a Christian home. That is a treasure that I want to pass along to my children.

—BABBIE MASON

[11] Then I saw a great white throne and Him who sat on it, from whose face the earth and the heaven fled away. And there was found no place for them. [12] And I saw the dead, small and great, standing before God, and books were opened. And another book was opened, which is the Book of Life. And the dead were judged according to their works, by the things which were written in the books. [13] The sea gave up the dead who were in it, and Death and Hades delivered up the dead who were in them. And they were judged, each one according to his works. [14] Then Death and Hades were cast into the lake of fire. This is the second death. [15] And anyone not found written in the Book of Life was cast into the lake of fire.

—REVELATION 20:11–15

*I see earth receding,*

*Heaven is opening,*

*God is calling, I must go.*

*If this is death, it is sweet.*

*This is my coronation day.*

—Dwight L. Moody

*"Do not be afraid; only believe."*

—Jesus of Nazareth
*(Mark 5:36)*

# Heaven Affects How We Die

Someday, somehow we'll all leave this life.

Many of us—especially the ill or aging—see the end of life approaching. We're finalizing our wills and insurance policies. We're savoring moments with loved ones. We're getting ready to move on.

Others of us—especially the young or healthy—may be surprised when life ends here, but we can still be prepared on the most important point, our certainty of Heaven through relationship with Jesus.

We can die with confidence in our future, and leave that final comfort of reunion to our loved ones.

But rest in peace? Who needs rest when we'll have new bodies and all of Heaven to explore!

# We Die with Confidence

"Peace I leave with you, My peace I give to you; not as the world gives
do I give to you. Let not your heart be troubled, neither let it be afraid.
You have heard Me say to you, 'I am going away and coming back to
you.' If you loved Me, you would rejoice because I said,
'I am going to the Father, for My Father is greater than I.'
"And now I have told you before it comes, that when it does come to
pass, you may believe."

—JOHN 14:27–29

My grandfather was the first one in my family who I ever had to surrender
to the dying part of living, and that loss made me begin to ask questions that
I had never asked before. I remember at his funeral ceremony, I kept wondering
if he was watching and if he could hear the tributes being paid to him. I
never had pondered those things. It had never mattered to me, but suddenly I
would think of him in the ensuing days and I would think, "Is he looking, is
he watching now, can he see us?" I began to wonder just what the steps were,
what the processes were from here to there.

—JANET PASCHAL

HEAVEN

*Be sure to celebrate my funeral scripturally and send*
*Hallelujahs all round. It is a better day than one's wedding day.*

—C. T. STUDD

I went with my pastor to a hospital to see a young woman who needed prayer. Earlier in her life she had worked with the youth at her church, but she got into drugs and became a prostitute to pay for her drug habit. They took her out of jail to put her in the hospital to die. There were sores all over her body, she weighed less than ninety pounds, and all she could do was moan. But her eyes were bright and alert. I saw a vibrant spirit trapped in a body that was dying. We prayed with her and asked her if she was ready to see Jesus. And she nodded, "Yes." Her eyes said, "Yes, I want to leave this frame, I want to leave this body and go to a new body and a new place." I stood there with tears running down my face, because of how separate the spirit is from the body. The spirit does not die.

—RUSS TAFF

*So now also Christ will be magnified in my body, whether by life or by death. For to me, to live is Christ, and to die is gain. But if I live on in the flesh, this will mean fruit from my labor; yet what I shall choose I cannot tell. For I am hard-pressed between the two, having a desire to depart and be with Christ, which is far better.*

—PHILIPPIANS 1:20–23

*Some day you will read in the papers that D. L. Moody*

*of East Northfield, is dead. Don't you believe a word of it!*

*At that moment I shall be more alive than I am now;*

*I shall have gone up higher, that is all, out of this old clay tenement*

*into a house that is immortal—a body that death cannot touch,*

*that sin cannot taint; a body fashioned like unto His glorious body.*

—DWIGHT L. MOODY

I think it is natural to have some fear of death, and I think it is normal for us to sit around and talk about going to Heaven. Certainly, I don't want to be on the next load going, but it amazes me that the people who are very near that journey are so at peace, which is a testimony to everyone around them that there is something out there. It seems like the Spirit moves in on them and they just have a quiet stillness and a ray about them. One of the last days that my grandmother was here, my mother looked at her and said, "Mom, what do you want us to do?" And she said, "Look, I am ready, your father is waiting on me, and I am ready to see Heaven. Don't hold me here and I will see you again later."

—BUDDY MULLINS

*Therefore we do not lose heart. Even though our outward man is perishing, yet the inward man is being renewed day by day.*

—2 CORINTHIANS 4:16

H E A V E N

# On Jordan's Stormy Banks I Stand

SAMUEL STENNETT, 1787

On Jordan's stormy banks I stand,
And cast a wishful eye
To Canaan's fair and happy land,
Where my possessions lie.

I am bound for the promised land,
I am bound for the promised land;
Oh who will come and go with me?
I am bound for the promised land.

When I shall reach that happy place,
I'll be forever blest,
For I shall see my Father's face,
And in His bosom rest.

# O COME, ANGEL BAND

## JEFFERSON HASCALL, 1860

*My latest sun is sinking fast, My race is nearly run;*
*My strongest trials now are past, My triumph is begun.*

*O come, angel band,*
*Come, and around me stand;*
*O bear me away on your snowy wings*
*To my immortal home.*

*I know I'm near the holy ranks Of friends and kindred dear;*
*I brush the dews on Jordan's banks: The crossing must be near.*

*I've almost gained my heavenly home, My spirit loudly sings;*
*Thy holy ones, behold, they come! I hear the noise of wings.*

Pelle and I had a dear pastor friend in Sweden who had taken gravely ill. For two weeks he had been in and out of a coma until one very memorable day. As his wife sat beside him, he jumped out of bed with his eyes wide open, threw his arms up and said, "Jesus! Praise music!" And then he fell back into his bed and he entered into Heaven. You see, he had been invited to a party, and peeking through the gate he caught sight of the Guest of honor, and heard the party music, and he had to go.

—EVIE KARLSSON

My father, Bob Benson, wrote these lines back when he didn't know any more about this than we do. "I used to think, loving life so greatly, that to die would be like leaving the party before the end. But now I know that the party is really happening somewhere else. That the light and the music escaping in snatches to make the pulse beat faster and the tempo quicken come from another place. And I know, too, that when I get there the music and the love and the praise will belong to him. And the music will never end."

—ROBERT BENSON

*He whose head is in Heaven*

*need not fear to put his foot in the grave.*

—MATTHEW HENRY

It was a deeply sobering day when I came to Carl's room in the hospital, knowing he had only a matter of hours to live. As I sat by his bedside, I asked, "Carl, how are you feeling?" A man of deep faith and commitment to Jesus Christ—and a very experienced and highly respected lighting director at CBS—he looked at me, his eyes misted slightly, and he said, "Pastor Jack, in my business it's the combination of lights, the skill of blending things together in order to create special effects—that's what the job is about. This morning I woke up and in the quiet of my heart, Jesus spoke to me and He said, 'Carl, how would you like to direct a sunset?'" There's something about the gentleness of Jesus and something about Him speaking to each of us at the specific point of our own interests and giftings, and how Heaven will amplify them to an entirely new dimension, all wrapped up in Carl's preparation to go home to Heaven.

—JACK HAYFORD

My father spent time in our home in the latter years of his life. Something happened during that time—that big flip in perspective, that same sort of thing that causes a nonbeliever to become a believer. Something like that happened to my Dad, when he was no longer concerned with the things of this world. Something flipped, and it was God preparing him to leave. Until that flip is made we enjoy life pretty well, and I think it is supposed to be enjoyed, but something eventually is going to happen and then make us realize that Heaven is a better place. Something happens that makes us ready for eternity, the corruptible becoming incorruptible.

—LARNELLE HARRIS

*The body of Benjamin Franklin/printer, like an old book,*

*its contents torn out. And stripped of its lettering and gilding,*

*lies here. Food for worms. But the work shall not be lost.*

*It will (as he believed) appear once more, in a new and more*

*beautiful edition, corrected and amended by the Author.*

—EPITAPH OF BENJAMIN FRANKLIN

"I never got to have dessert," she sighed, as they wheeled her by stretcher from the table where she had grown faint. That was the last thing I ever heard her say. Two days later we received the news that she had died. The long struggle with her failing body finally over. And I have a strange feeling that somebody somewhere, maybe with a sense of humor and irony, saw to it that she eventually got her dessert. God has an uncanny way of saving the best for last.

—SUZANNE JENNINGS

Humans fear the unknown, period. Much of the good stuff here on earth is really good, and we hate to walk away from it. I just wish we could understand that when we die, we are only walking away from the pain. We are walking away from only the destructive stuff, the broken pieces, all of that. The truly good things here will only be better in Heaven.

—GLORIA GAITHER

# The Veil Will Be Lifted

*Now we see things imperfectly as in a poor mirror, but then we will see everything with perfect clarity. All that I know now is partial and incomplete, but then I will know everything completely, just as God knows me now.*

—I CORINTHIANS 13:12

My daughter Amy taught me a great lesson about Heaven when she was little. She asked me, "Do you think we go to Heaven or does Heaven really come to us?" She went on to explain, "I think Heaven is all around us now. Being here holds Heaven back, but when we die, Heaven can just come on in." There is as much Heaven around us now as there will ever be if we have eyes for it, because eternity starts when we give ourselves to God. And Amy had it right—nothing will interrupt eternity. Death only releases more of it, but it is not another place, another time. It is here, it is now. Scripture refers to the stuff of life as a veil, and with each Homecoming event and the more people we lose, the more I am convinced that the curtain is very sheer. Very sheer!

—GLORIA GAITHER

*We have this hope as an anchor for the soul, firm and secure. It enters the inner sanctuary behind the curtain, where Jesus, who went before us, has entered on our behalf.*

HEBREWS 6:19–20, NIV

Heaven, at last, the dark glass is broken and I can see clearly a glory so bright that all my attention is taken off me.

—DUDLEY HALL

# Someone I Love Is Dying

### Gloria Gaither

I wrote a prayer while watching Bill's mom die. I sat with my mother the day that she died. I was also at the births of our grandchildren, and I couldn't believe how similar the process of death was to the process of being born. Like false labor, you think you are going to lose them. Then they get their second wind and stay a little longer. Eventually though, comes the moment, and it doesn't matter whether you are catching a child coming down the chute or whether the veil is lifting so you can place the hand of someone you love into the hand of God. For a moment you see a flash of glory, and that moment, that flash, the veil lifting between here and the other side, will change you forever. Birth and death are very similar, eternal moments.

*Lord,*

Someone I love is dying. I've learned that dying doesn't happen all of a sudden any more than being born does. It is a process. There are signs and indications, sometimes false contractions and pain. But the exact time can't be predicted. Coming into and going out of this world is not an easy thing. These are adventures like no other in the life between. No one can accurately chart their courses or predict the experience. Birth and death are unique to each person.

Thank you Lord, for the privilege of walking through this passage. As hard and sometimes agonizing as it is, I wouldn't miss it. To touch eternity so intimately, to hand off the hand I am holding to the very hand of God changes me. The glitter of glory lands on my face, too, and changes the way I see things. I remember watching my grandbabies being born, emerging from the embryotic fluids all powdered with the rich white coating of birth. I wanted to turn my face away from the agony that my daughter was experiencing, but the fascination of that moment and her need for someone who had been there kept me so engaged. A thousand horses couldn't have pulled me away. My love for my child and her child helped me.

Now the labor of death tells me that soon the passage door is opening to a place where an aging body will not be needed anymore. I feel that what seems to be going away from here, in reality is a birth into a new place. Someone will be waiting and reading the signs and anticipating. The door will open just long enough for me to glimpse the eternal and for them to have a strange moment of remembering another time, another place. As Heaven sent us one of its sweet treasures when those babies were born, we are now sending Heaven a treasure we have held dear, entrusting our loved one to other arms, other hearts.

Thank You, Lord. Only at a birth or a death do we get real about life. Help me remember.

# HEA

*The Glory of God!*

# VEN

*H*eaven is everything good that ever was, and ever will be.

It is all joy, all glory, all power, all worship, all love, all peace, all wholeness, all acceptance, all health, all intimacy, all pleasure, all celebration, all family, all beauty—all beyond imagining, all forever!

Heaven is the undiluted presence of God, and we're all invited to join Him there.

Heaven is a choice. We hope it is yours.

*Dear God,*

*We pray that this book is a blessing*

*to each reader. We pray that You have opened*

*their eyes more to the glory that You are,*

*the relationship You offer, and the home that*

*You promise. Thank you for Your hope.*

*We thank you for the ways You bless us here,*

*and we look forward to the Homecoming in Heaven*

*with You and all our loved ones.*

*In Jesus' Name,*

*Amen*

# *A Celebration of* Heaven

 ill & Gloria Gaither and their Homecoming Friends® invite you to explore Heaven with them in their new videos, *Heaven* and *Going Home*.

Going where no Homecoming projects have gone before, these two new recordings celebrate the glorious hope of Heaven. In these groundbreaking videos, Bill Gaither realizes his longtime dream of bringing together music, dialogue, readings, and reflections about the world to come. Authors, theologians, and others join Bill & Gloria Gaither and their Homecoming Friends with profound truths spoken about the ultimate Homecoming.

*Available wherever music is sold.*

# ACKNOWLEDGEMENTS

p.18    "Hope," Written by Gloria Gaither
© 2002, 2003 Gloria Gaither. All rights reserved. Used by permission.

p. 19    "When All of God's Singers Get Home," Written by Gloria Gaither
© 1995 Gloria Gaither. All rights reserved. Used by permission.

p. 25    "Beyond the Sunset," Written by Virgil P. Brock, Blanche Kerr Brock
© 1936, renewed 1964 by the Rodeheaver Company (a division of Word, Inc.).
All rights reserved. Used by permission.

p. 27    "Look for Me," Written by Rusty Goodman
© 1982 First Monday Music (a div. of Word, Inc.).
All rights reserved. Used by permission.

p. 28    "Knowing You'll Be There," Written by Suzanne Jennings, Michael Sykes
© 2002 Townsend and Warbucks Music, Mal 'N Al Music. Adm. By Gaither Copyright Management.
All rights reserved. Used by permission.

p. 31    "I Don't Belong (Sojourner's Song)," Written by Gloria Gaither, Buddy Greene
© 1990 Gaither Music Company, Rufus Music, SpiritQuest Music. Adm. By Gaither Copyright Management.
All rights reserved. Used by permission.

p. 34    "Sweet Beulah Land," Written by Squire Parsons, Jr.
© 1979 Kingsmen Publishing Company. Adm. By Brentwood—Benson Music Publishing, Inc.
All rights reserved. Used by permission.

p. 38    "What a Day That Will Be," Written by Jim Hill.
© 1955, renewed 1983 by Ben Speer Music. Adm. by Integrated Copyright Group, Inc.
All rights reserved. Used by permission.

p. 44    "Heaven Will Be All of It," Written by Gloria Gaither
© 2003 Gloria Gaither. All rights reserved. Used by permission.

p. 49    "Jesus, I Heard You Had a Big House," Written by William J. & Gloria Gaither
© 1975 Gaither Music Company. All rights reserved. Used by permission.

p. 50    "I Couldn't Begin to Tell You,"Written by Albert E. Brumley
© 1940 Stamps—Baxter Music. Adm. By Brentwood—Benson Music Publishing, Inc.
All rights reserved. Used by permission.

p. 70    "Next Time We Meet," Written by Gloria Gaither
© 2003 Gloria Gaither. All rights reserved. Used by permission.

p. 80    "I Then Shall Live," Written by Gloria Gaither
© 1981 William J. Gaither. All rights reserved. Used by permission.

p. 83    "Because He Lives," Written by William J. & Gloria Gaither
© 1971 William J. Gaither. All rights reserved. Used by permission.

p. 84    "It's Not About Now," Written by Gloria Gaither
© 2001, 2003 Gloria Gaither. All rights reserved. Used by permission.

p. 96    "Canaanland Is Just in Sight," Written by Jeff Gibson
© 1983 Bridge Building Music, Inc. (Adm. By Brentwood—Benson Music Publishing.)
All rights reserved. Used by permission.

p. 117    "I Never Got to Have Dessert," Written by Suzanne Jennings
© 2003 Suzanne Jennings. All rights reserved. Used by permission.

p. 120    "Someone I Love Is Dying," from *Prayers and Songs for the New Millennium*, Written by Gloria Gaither
© 2003 Gloria Gaither. All rights reserved. Used by permission.